The incredible Qualities of Lord Shiva:

Life lessons to learn from Shiva

By Santosh Gairola

DEDICATION

I dedicate this book to my family: my father **Mr. M.N Gairola**, my mother **Basanti Gairola**, and sisters **Beena, & Reena**. Without their support and encouragement writing, this book wouldn't be possible for me.

After that, I would like to dedicate this book to my lovely audience. I like to thank everyone who assisted me in my good times and bad times.

Life is beautiful because I have so many loving and caring people around me. I like to give a shout out to some of the names who are always supportive and caring towards my work.

Sumit Sao, Saurabh Tiwari, Santanu Debnath, Nirmala Santhakumar, Sue-Ann Bubacz, Rahul Bhichher, Navin Rao, Harleena Singh, Ryan Biddulph, Erika R. Mohssen-Beyk, Vishwajeet Kumar, Akash Singh, Tarun Kashyap, Ankit Rawat, Anurag Guleria,

Ranjay, Bishnu Saran, Deeksha Mamgain, Grish Chandra, Mukul, Manish, Jaypal Thakor, Kishor Srinivas, Parveender Lamba, Saurabh Panwar, Shivam Kumar, Yasar Arafath Shruti Pradhan, and Sayara St Clair.

Thank you, guys for always being so supportive and kind to my work. Life is beautiful because of the presence of Shiva tattva in it.

I bow down to Lord Shiva and chant Om Namah Shivaya.

Om gan ganpataye namah

Preface

Lord Shiva is one of the most loved Lords in Sanatan Dharma. Whenever someone explores the qualities of Lord Shiva, they get ecstatic in their devotion. Every virtue of Shiva is charming and beautiful in all primary aspects.

Therefore, learning and practicing these characteristics can transform your life. You can sense Shiva's consciousness within you in any form whether you find him as your friend, Guru, or even divine father.

Shiva is infinite, and by following the teachings of Shiva, you can also become limitless like him. After implementing the qualities of Lord Shiva, you will start experiencing blissfulness all around you.

Most importantly, you will learn the meaning of truth, strength, moksha, kindness, love, vairagya, reliability, and inner peace.

Santosh Gairola

Contents

Introduction

Om Namah Shivaya

Sanatan Dharma has many gods and goddesses, but primarily Brahma, Vishnu, and Mahesh are the most influential.

They are known as Trinity in the Vedic culture. But for a substantial segment of humanity Lord Shiva is the most attractive in them.

Shiva is Chidanand Swaroop, and there are many forms of Maheshwara Shiva. He is a destroyer as well as known for his kindness.

How is it possible that someone known as the greatest destroyer is also known for his generosity?

How does Lord Shiva manage these two opposite aspects of his persona?

To figure out the answer to the above question, firstly, we need to understand that Lord Shiva is everywhere.

He is in the anarchy of the world, as well as in the meditation of a sage. It depends on the seeker how they want to find him?

Now, the question comes, who is Shiva, and how can we understand his various perspectives?

The book: 'incredible qualities of Lord Shiva' will help you understand Shiva as Mahadev.

After finishing this book, you will realize why Shiva devotees love him so much?

So let's get started without wasting any time further.

Lord Shiva is supreme; he is the highest form of divinity revered as eternal God. He is the compassionate one who gave the blessing to Bhagiratha.

Due to that blessing, **Goddess Ganga** descended into the mother earth. Today, a large segment of humanity is flourishing under her blessings.

It is fascinating to know that in a broader aspect, there is no founder of Hinduism. Indeed there is no such religion known as Hinduism.

The actual name is Sanatan Dharma. The term Sanatan means eternal, and dharma represents responsibility towards humanity.

There are different branches in the eternal dharma, which glorifies diversity in the ancient tradition.

It is the reason Sanatan dharma is known as the peaceful belief system in human history. It focuses more on inner peace, moksha, and liberation from worldly suffering.

Sanatan dharma teaches the philosophy of coexistence and tolerance. There is complete freedom for everyone, which helps them to find their inner peace.

That is what makes it beautiful and sovereign. Hence, Sanatan dharma is a lifestyle and not a religion.

Shiva Shankara is the primary godhead in Sanatan Dharma. Without whom the imagination of the trinity is impossible.

Trinity is the trilogy of Lord Brahma, Lord Vishnu, and Mahadev.

Lord Shiva is known as **Mahadev**, which means the generous God of all realms.

Shiva is Nirguna as well as Sarguna, and there are no traditional rituals to worship him.

The only requirement for pleasing Lord Shiva is keeping genuine reverence in the heart for Lord Shiva.

Lord Shiva is free from all restrictions, and everybody is free to worship him. You can worship him in any form.

He is a father, the loving husband of Goddess Shakti, and a friend of Lord Vishnu.

Goddess Shakti manifested herself in the physical reality to marry Lord Shiva. But their wedlock remained unsuccessful due to Daksha's ego.

To balance the functioning of the world, Adishakti again personified herself as Goddess Parvati.

Later, Shiva and Parvati married with the Vedic rituals. There is so much that the modern generation can learn from Shiva and Parvati.

Both Shiva and Parvati are inseparable from each other. Their love is pure and unconditional.

Although, Lord Shiva operates as the destroyer of the darkness in the trinity but there is a bigger picture of it in which Lord Shiva is a creator, preserver, and destroyer of the world.

Everything emerges from Shiva and gets back into Shiva at the end of the Kalpa. It is the reason Shiva is also known as Maha Sunya, which means someone with no endpoints. Lord Shiva's Lingam is the manifestation of that infiniteness.

Shiva is always calm and known for living a highly ascetic life in forests and mountains. He is known for giving liberation to Jiva from all the agonies. Shiva always served justice to all without discriminating against anyone.

Every living being is categorized, as Pashu, whether they are animals, plants, or humans. Shiva is their Nath, which means their master. Hence, Shiva is called **Pashupati Nath**, the Lord of everyone, including Ghosts, Sages, humans, and deities.

In the primary creator form, Shiva is **Hiranyagarbha.** It means the cosmic spore of the universal phenomena. It is the place where the process of creation started first.

Lord Shiva is omnipresent, invincible, incredible, incomparable, Infinite, and Aradhya of Lord Vishnu. Yes, Lord Shiva is known as **Vishnu Vallbha** by Vishnu devotees.

The name Vishnu Vallbha signifies that Shiva is most dear to

Lord Vishnu.

Shiva is beyond the perception of the human mind. Even Vedas and Upanishads cannot describe the complete impeccable glory of

Maheshwara.

Vedas state that Shiva is Mahadev, which means great God of the world. Everything about Lord Shiva is grand and cannot be described in the words.

Shiva is the moksha giver who is free from all sorts of disorders.

Mount Kailash is the abode of Lord Shiva, which is a sacred place for all the Hindus. In his physical form, he adorns the white silvery crescent lightning on his head.

Lord Shiva is the true definition of Supremacy, and the third eye over the middle of the forehead represents his governance to the universe.

There is no one like Shiva Shankar; when the armies of deities and asuras got scared with the emergence of the Halahal (cosmic poison).

At that fragile moment, everyone prayed to Shiva. The greatest Lord Shiva drank that cosmic Halahal to protect the universe from its adverse effect.

The poison was so strong that it turned Shiva's throat in blue. That's how Shiva became Neelkantha, which means the man with a Bluethroat.

There is no beginning and end of Lord Shiva. He is immortal who never takes birth on earth like other deities and celestial beings.

It is captivating that Shiva is the only Lord who exists in bilateral nature in which his supreme form is attributeless and known as SadaShiva. The other form is naturally attractive. But both forms are one in the higher state.

Hence, when we talk about Shiva to a deeper extent, Shiva means someone who doesn't have any physical reality. But all sorts of physical actualities dwell within him.

Sadashiva manifested himself as **Shiva Shankara** so that ordinary minds could get his personification on their minds.

Everything connected to Shiva's physical form is remarkable.

The physical form of Shiva is known as auspicious Shiva. That benignant form of Shiva is Shankar, which is the prime reason for every reason.

In this book, I have discussed some of the extraordinary qualities of Lord Shiva. Knowing them is a blissful experience.

By implementing these qualities, you can build a strong personality. Learning these virtues will transform your life positively. They will help you to achieve what is impossible for you now.

Dear friend, if you love reading more such content. We have more for you. Please feel free to grab these as well. We are thankful for all your support and love. It means a lot.

More Kindle ebooks for respective Marketplaces

Check out author's other books available on the Amazon Store.

1. The Love Story of Lord Shiva and Goddess Shakti: A tale of divine Love
2. The benefits of Om Namah Shivaya Chanting: Lord Shiva Mantra
3. The Magnificent Shiva: Why there is no one like Lord Shiva?
4. Mahadev, the Lord of the Lords

These ebooks are available for all the respective marketplaces.

More Paperback Books for the respective Marketplaces

1. The Love Story of Lord Shiva and Goddess Shakti: A tale of divine Love
2. The benefits of Om Namah Shivaya Chanting: Lord Shiva Mantra
3. The Magnificent Shiva: Why there is no one like Lord Shiva?
4. Maryada Purushottam Rama: The story of Lord Rama
5. Mahadev, the Lord of the Lords.

These books are available for all the respective marketplaces.

Please don't forget to follow me on Amazon, Instagram, and Facebook. Details are available in the author segment of the book.

Regards santosh Gairola

Thank you.

Rudra Gayatri Mantra

Om Tatpurushay Vidmahe
Mahaadevaay Dheemahi
Tanno Rudrah Prachodayaat

Om Namah Shivaya

CHAPTER 1

The auspicious appearance of Shiva

Nagendra haraya Trilochanaya, Basmanga ragaya maheswaraya,

Nithyaya shudhaya digambaraya, Tasmai nakaraya namashivaya

Lord Shiva's name gives the sense of purity, calmness, limitless strength, and infinite knowledge. He is the Lord of the world who lives on Mount Kailash as the ruler of the world.

He is one of the most loved Lords in ancient culture. From demons to deities, Lord Shiva is dear to all. Everyone has their reason to worship Shiva.

The whole world calls him Trilokinatha, who loves smearing cremation ground ashes on his body. The outer appearance of Shiva is grand, and everything about Shiva's look is just winsome.

Shiva looks tough from the outside but too compassionate from the inner side. You can easily find Shiva's devotees near the bank of the holy river Ganga. They might be meditating on Shiva's name or maybe chanting Har Har Mahadev. Once you get to know about the qualities of Shiva, you get mesmerized by him.

Let's find out what is exceptional about Lord Shiva and why yogis, **Aghoris**, sages, ghosts, and celestial beings adore him so much.

On asking a Himalayan Yogi on the bank of Ganga, who is Shiva?

He will confidently reply to you after lifting his hands toward the sky and say Shiva is Param Brahman, the remover of all sufferings.

Nectar flows through his Jata. He is God of Gods, Mahadev.

Now let's dig into detail what makes Shiva grand in every aspect.

1 Shiva's long and thick hairs [Jatadharaya]

Lord Shiva is called Jatadharaya. It means Shiva has long and thick matted hairs coiled where goddess Ganga resides and her water flows downwards through Lord Shiva's hair.

The matted hairs of Lord Shiva are part of the Yogic culture. But it has deep spiritual meaning as well. The long thick hairs represent the limitless worldly desires of the human.

Shiva's coiled hair symbolizes that man must control his worldly desires to live a happy life. Otherwise, the entire happiness of the world will not be enough for that person.

2 The flow of Ganga's water over his head

The flow of Ganga on Shiva's head represents the concept of Gyan Ganga. Knowledge is power. It means the stream of knowledge should keep flowing on a person's head.

Knowledge is an intangible asset which no one can steal from you. The constant flow of information is essential for living an impactful life.

The beautiful thing about learning is nobody can take it away from you

—B. B. King.

River Ganga has given much significance in the Vedic scripture. These scriptures describe the purity and medicinal qualities of the river Ganga.

Hence, like Ganga, a person should keep feeding only positive thoughts to the mind.

Ganga is not just a river to us; Ganga is our divine mother who nourishes every spectrum of our life.

In Hinduism, the river Ganga is believed to be our divine mother. Almost every Hindu keeps Ganga's water in their home for spiritual cleansing.

How unfortunate is that, we as a human polluted the elixir given to us by Shiva.

3 Crescent over the head

There is a beautiful white crescent over Lord Shiva's head. It is also one of the reasons that Lord Shiva is called Chandrashekhar.

It is one of the most charming forms of Lord Shiva. But there is also a deeper meaning associated with the crescent over Lord Shiva's head.

The crescent represents the importance of Kaal Chakra, which means the wheel of time. Crescent over Shiva's head symbolizes that Shiva is beyond every physical dimension.

Kaal is an ancient term, which stands for different aspects of physical realities like time, death, space, and energy. It is the humans or other beings that are directly dependent on Kaal.

Kaal destroys everyone; we mature with time and die in the end. But it never stops for anyone. In that way, time keeps flowing with its speed.

Only Shiva is free from these limitations. Shiva is Mahakaal, the one who is beyond time, space, death, and other dimensions.

Lord Shiva is the one who has conquered everything and lives in the highest dimension.

No one ever reached that highest dimension. Even Lord Vishnu is in the second-highest dimension, followed by Lord Brahma in the third.

There is one more thing that makes the crescent unique over Shiva's head.

As we know that the moon's surface is cold as compared to other celestial bodies in our solar system.

Therefore **moon over Shiva's head** also implies that a person should keep patience in every situation. Only a calm mind can lead to a prosperous life.

4 The third eye on the middle of the forehead

If I ask you, how many eyes do you have? You will reply, what kind of question is that obviously, you have two eyes, but what if I tell you that you have three eyes, not two. The thing that I'm saying is also medically proven.

I know this is a little weird, but trust me, what I am saying to you. Your third eye is not as visible as your two eyes. It is a spiritual eye and lies inside your forehead.

Our eyes are the visual apparatus that we use to perceive the information from our surroundings. Through our eyes, we come to know what is happening around us.

The information that we get, our brain works on that basis.

These two eyes help us to get an external view, what is happening in the world. But what is happening inside? How to perceive inward reality?

It might be interesting to know that every human being has an additional visual apparatus. It is called the spiritual eye or third eye.

The job of the third eye is to see the inward dimension. Through this eye, people could know what is happening in their inner world.

Hence, People whose third eye is awake; those people can heal themselves.

Yes, they can figure out their dysfunctional organs, tissues, cells and heal them internally without any external medicines. In Medical terms, the concept comes under the category of **neuroplasticity**.

Similarly, **Lord Shiva's spiritual third eye** on the middle of the forehead represents his yogic power.

You only need to awake your inner consciousness. Once you have achieved your inner Shiva, you will become limitless as Shiva.

 In humans, the Pineal gland governs the spiritual eye. Now think for a moment how intelligent the ancient yogis were.

These people were aware of modern science. Do you know, by chanting Vedic mantras, they had the science to modify the DNA structures?

It is still possible today through ancient Yoga and meditation practice. You can unlock the limitless capabilities of your third eye.

The Third eye is also known **as Agna Chakra** in Shiva Yoga. It is the second most potent Chakra, whereas **Sahasrara** is the most influential Chakra, where goddess Shakti meets Shiva.

5 Snake Vasuki on the neck

There is a giant snake on Lord Shiva's neck coiled three times. The snake's name is **Vasuki**, the king of the serpent community.

The three coils of the Snake around Shiva's neck represent the Kundalini Shakti of the individual. Snake **Vasuki** on Bholenath's neck implies that Shiva is the master of the Kundalini Shakti.

The three coils of the snake also represent three dimensions of time Past, Present, and Future.

It also depicts the three Gunas of the individual Rajas, Sattva and Tamas. The essential thing to understand from that is Shiva is free from all three Gunas.

There is another aspect of Shiva carrying a snake on the neck. As we all know that snakes are poisonous, and lots of people consider them inauspicious. These creatures are disrespected and mercilessly killed by humans.

Shiva wrapping Snakes as the necklace helped these creatures to get back their lost respect. Now, whenever people see snakes in Shivalayas, instead of killing them. They admire them, glorify them.

6 Shiva smears cremation ground ashes

Being Aghor is one of the attractive characteristics of Lord Shiva. Ghor means extreme, and Aghor implies he is simply uncomplicated. He loves everyone without differentiating in between them.

Lord Shiva is non-materialistic Lord who dwells in the cremation ground. Shiva sits on the cremation ground for meditation and applies the dead body's ashes.

We all know that Shiva is Bhootnath, which means Lord of Panch Mahabhootas. These Mahabhoot are the five primary elements of life.

Shiva controls them. Shiva is also known for establishing the balance of the positive and negatives energies.

Lord Shiva smearing cremation ground ashes also gives a meaningful message to the world that this entire creation is destroyable, then, why do we as a human have so much attachment with the mundane world?

Ghostly distorted creatures of cremation grounds roam around him and worship him, and admire him. These creatures are considered inauspicious.

Everyone tried to mistreat them. Only Lord Shiva gave them refuge so that they could attain their inner peace and not harm others.

7 Shiva Sitting over tiger Skin and meditating

Lord Shiva Sitting over the tiger skin represents that Shiva is the destroyer of the darkness and all the sinfulness. Shiva liberates people from their past sins and purifies their souls by removing arrogance, Kaam, Krodh, Moh, and Maya.

Such weakness doesn't let you explore your full potential to make your life blissful. You will keep running behind materialistic worldly greed.

Hence, there is so much we could learn from Lord Shiva. The other most incredible thing that you can learn from Lord Shiva is his unconditional love for Goddess Parvati.

Let's move further to know in detail.

CHAPTER 2

Ideal Lover and Best husband

By chance, if you ever get interested in learning the meaning of true love, you must read the love story of Lord Shiva and Goddess Shakti. You will realize why Lord Shiva is given so much significance in Hinduism?

The story of Lord Shiva and Goddess Parvati is the Story of faith and Love. Indeed, it is a legendary story of trusting the partner and sacrificing for that beloved.

He is almighty but acted like a human for goddess happiness. Similarly, you will like how a princess could leave her luxurious life for a Vairagi, who has nothing to give her.

Sanyasi had nothing except a bull named Nandi and a few distorted creatures as his Gans.

Lord is known for living an extremely harsh life in the mountains of the Himalayas. But goddess Parvati left her everything to marry Lord Shiva and adapted the same lifestyle Lord has.

Many times, they got separated from each other for the prosperity of the world. But they meet again with the same love. Their story reveals that trust, affection, and love are the fundamental blocks of any relationship.

Hence, if you are ready to become a husband like Shiva; then, you will realize that your loving wife will transform herself as your Shakti.

Indeed, if you compare Lord Shiva and Goddess Parvati in their origin, you will notice that Shiva is supreme who never takes birth.

Whereas Goddess Parvati was mortal, so the crucial point is, Shiva helped Goddess Parvati to achieve her sublime divinity.

Lord Shiva is unique in all aspects, and almost every unmarried girl wants to get married to a man who has the qualities of Shiva.

Goddess Parvati is the most renowned form of Adi Shakti. Many times goddess Shakti manifested herself to marry just Lord Shiva.

She has various names like Uma, Aparana, Gauri, and Annapoorna. Shiva and Parvati make an ideal pair worshipped all over the world. A simple smile of Gauri is enough to win Shiva's heart.

Once goddess AdiShakti in the form of Goddess, Sati gave her life in the Daksha Yagna. She gave her life in the Daksha Yagna to protect Shiva's honor because her father, Daksha, was abusing the name of Lord Shiva in that Yagna.

As the loving spouse of Shiva, she couldn't bear the insult of Lord Shiva, so she decides to leave that human torso. The loss of Sati melted the heart of Shiva.

The rage was tremendous. Therefore to punish Daksha, Shiva destroyed the entire kingdom of Daksha as Veerbhadra, the angry form of Shiva. Later, Shiva beheaded Daksha for that sin, and he became Vairagi again.

Shiva's love was so pure for goddess Sati. Hence, Lord Shiva roamed in the entire universe carrying the dead body of goddess Sati.

During Shiva's separation with Sati, Lord Shiva experienced the incredible pain of separation.

To detach Shiva from that agony, Lord Vishnu cuts Goddess Sati's body into 51 parts with Sudarshan Chakra. After that, Shiva almost decided to lose his divinity in the pain of losing Sati.

But for the welfare of the world, Shiva regained his godhead and took Samadhi in a dark cave. To complete the wedlock, AdiShakti again manifested herself as Goddess Parvati.

She meditated on Shiva and performed rigorous austerity to achieve him as her husband. It was not only Goddess Parvati's penance on Mahadev. It was also Lord Shiva's sacrifice for Goddess Shakti, due to which Shiva accepted Vairagya again.

Lord Shiva indulged himself into a deep meditation till Shakti reappears as Goddess Parvati. The holy river Ganga was willing to marry Shiva, but Shiva restricted Ganga.

Lord Shiva said that he couldn't marry any other lady except his Shakti. Goddess Ganga respected the decision of Shiva, and in honor of Ganga, Shiva gave her an appropriate position on his matted coiled hairs.

On the other side, due to intense penance on Shiva, Goddess Parvati's soft skin becomes dark. But she wins the heart of Lord Shiva with that penance.

 Shiva appears to meet goddess Parvati, and the goddess becomes white again. With so much love and affection for Parvati in his heart, Shiva gives her new names Gauri, Uma, and Aparna.

Goddess Parvati accepts the metaphor given to her by Lord Shiva with humility. She also requested Shiva to ask for her hand from her father, Himavan.

She expresses her views to Shiva that she wants to get married with all the Vedic rituals. Despite being the Lord of Lords just for the happiness of Parvati, Shiva fulfilled all his promises given to Goddess Parvati. They were married with all the Vedic rituals.

The story of Shiva and Parvati explains that both have immense love for each other. Parvati is so caring for Shiva, and Shiva admires the virtues of Goddess Parvati.

After the Grand wedding of Shiva and Parvati, Goddess Parvati was slightly upset. Shiva acknowledged Parvati's pain of separating from her family.

For the happiness of Parvati, Shiva gets ready to leave his Kailash to stay with Parvati in Himavan's palace.

Shiva told Parvati that she doesn't need to leave her family, as Shiva himself is ready to live at Himavan palace as the son-in-law. Mahadev gets overwhelmed, and a few tears fall from Shiva's eyes by saying that.

That makes Parvati realize how much Shiva cares for her. Parvati wipes out the tears of Shiva, and to protect the honor of Mahadev, Parvati gets ready to leave her father's palace with Shiva.

Therefore, this explains that Shiva and Goddess Parvati have immense love for each other. Shiva has made goddess his strength. Shambhu includes her in making every decision.

Shiva is not just the spouse of Parvati; Shiva is a friend and Guru as well. Someone she can trust blindly.

Shiva's love for Goddess Parvati is unconditional and eternal. Goddess Parvati and Shiva are complementary to each other.

1. Gauri loves Shiva's charming look described above in the previous chapter.
2. Sangini of Shiva cherishes Shiva's immense love for her. She calls him Bhole Nath with love.
3. Uma admires Shiva as her loving husband, friend, and Guru.
4. Parvati shares the unshakable faith in the relationship with Shiva.
5. Bhole is too polite every time talking to goddess Parvati.
6. Maheswari cannot accept anyone's influence except Shiva.
7. Yogeswar Shiva respects Uma's every decision, and she knows it.
8. Shiva depicted goddess as his strength, not his weakness.
9. Shiva admires Parvati in all forms like Mahakali, Annapoorna.

Shiva's Love for Goddess Parvati is so strong, which is incomparable to anything else. Shiva helped Goddess Parvati come out of human limitations to attain her highest form of Adishakti through Yoga, Dhayan, Kundalini, Mantra, Veda Saar, and Tantra.

Goddess Parvati's Love is also not lesser than Shiva's love. To bring Lord Shiva out from dispassion, Adishakti personified herself as Parvati. She introduced Shiva to worldly traditions.

CHAPTER 3

Shiva represents Gender Equality

The most spectacular thing in Sanatan dharma is it honors women's contributions in our daily life. Shiva's Ardhnarishwar form is the best proof of it.

Lord Shiva's qualities give him an edge over the other deities and present him as one of the most prominent lords. The brilliant thing about Lord Shiva is the way; he manages his family and loves his consort, Goddess Parvati.

Goddess Shakti is an integral part of Shiva; she nurtures Shiva. In the broader aspect, goddess Parvati is the energy of Shiva; she helps Shiva in establishing balance in the world.

You cannot assume Shiva and Shakti separately. Shiva is Rudra, and Parvati is Rudrani. Both are a flux of the same energy, which is known as Shiva's Ardhnarishwar form. Whenever someone says Ardhnarishwar Shiva, it means half Shiva and half Shakti.

Here Shakti means goddess Parvati (the human form of the Adishakti).

Lord Shiva Ardhnarishwara's form is the balance of masculine and feminine forms within every individual. It is also known as the union of opposite energies.

Shiva is the Adipurush, which means the first male or Alpha male. And goddess Parvati is Prakriti (Mother Nature).

Shiva's Ardhnarishwar form is the most admired personification of Shiva all over the world. The Ardhnarishwar form symbolizes Shiva as the complete Lord in all the perspectives. In which the process of creation and destruction both dwells within him.

When someone genuinely studies Shiva's Ardhnarishwar form, they figure out a few points about Shiva.

1. Shiva Ardhnarishwar form is the Symbolism of gender equality.
2. Ardhnarishwar represents the purest form of love.
3. The balance of masculine and feminine energies within Kundalini.
4. Purush and Prakriti are contemporary to each other.
5. The flux of Dark energy and Dark matter.

In that way, there could be various prospects of that. Lord Shiva is known for taking care of everyone.
Shiva never did partiality with anyone. It is one of the reasons from Ravana to Lord Rama everyone worshipped him as Supreme consciousness.

On the Other hand, when it comes to gender equality, Shiva has given equal rights to goddess Parvati.

She resides in the Vam Bhaag of Shiva, which means goddess Parvati is Vamangi to Shiva.

Goddess sits on the left side of Shiva and takes active participation in every decision making. Shiva never does anything without consulting Gauri. Mahadev is the KanthHaar of Parvati, which means the Necklace of goddess Parvati.

Shiva is AdiYogi in the Yogic culture and resides in the highest state of consciousness. And goddess dwells as the Shakti in the base of the person. Kundalini yoga describes the power as the goddess energy stored in the serpent form.

When a Yogic person starts activating the Kundalini Shakti, it gets energized into the base Chakra known as Muladhara. The energy (Shakti) reaches the top chakra passing through every chakra to merge into Shiva at Sahasrara chakra.

Therefore, when energy gets awake within a yogi, Shiva and Shakti get intensified in them. It is the reason a true Yogi cannot separate Shiva and Shakti.

There is another aspect of Shiva and Shakti. As we all know, Shiva is Adipurusha, and Parvati is the Prakriti. Purush cannot do anything without Prakriti, and similarly, Prakriti needs Purush.

They are complementary to each other. At the cosmic level, the world has risen from nothingness. And at the end of the Kalpa, everything dissolves into the same voidness.

When someone explores the Vedic literature, they find out that Shiva-Shakti is Dark matter and Dark energy there.

Our universe contains only 4 percent available matter and 96 percent Dark energy. The Ardhnarishwar representation of Shiva symbolizes the flux of that Dark matter and Dark energy.

There is a story that explains why Shiva is known as Ardhnarishwar?

There was a devotee of Lord Shiva whose name was Bhringi. He was one of the extreme devotees of Lord Shiva. It means his reverence was limited to Shiva only. Every day Sage used to meditate on Shiva. But he never worshipped goddess Parvati, the consort of Lord Shiva.

Although Sage Bhringi's devotions were genuine for Shiva, the problem was he understood Shiva and goddess Parvati as two different identities. One day, while worshipping Shiva, he decided to do Parikrama of Shiva's Kailash.

[Parikrama is a ritual of moving clockwise around an object.]

After reaching there, he changed his mind to do Parikrama of Shiva instead of Kailash.

For that purpose, he reached the abode of Shiva. Sage Bhringi saw Shiva sitting with goddess Parvati, as Sage was the devotee of Shiva, and not of goddess Parvati.

He was not willing to do the Parikrama ritual of Shiva with goddess Parvati. He requests the goddess to leave Shiva for a few moments so he could perform the Parikrama ritual.

Goddess Parvati noticed the weird behavior of the sage, Bhringi. She rejected the request of Bhringi and sat closer to Shiva.

Sage Bhringi was stubborn; he decided to take the appearance of a snake and do Parikrama instantly without letting the goddess know.

On the other side, Lord Shiva was observing everything happening on Mount Kailash but stayed calm. After watching the actions of Sage Bhringi, Shiva semi-merged Parvati within him and sage Bhringi gets surprised.

Lord Shiva presented himself as Ardhnarishwar as half Shiva and half Parvati. Due to that, sage Bhringi became helpless; he still did not accept Shiva and Parvati as one.

Sage Bhringi was desperate to separate them. He took the appearance of a rat, and he started biting the joints of Shiva and Parvati. He was trying hard to separate them.

When Parvati saw a rat trying to separate them, Adishakti became angry at the sage. Adishakti cursed sage that whatever body he has gained from his mother will leave him immediately.

As Shiva tantra says, people get bones & flesh from their father, and blood & other attributes from their mother.

After the curse, sage falls on the ground and realizes his mistake. Goddess Parvati is equivalently kind-hearted as Shiva. She accepts the apology of the sage. Now, after the curse, sage was not able to stand on his feet.

Ardhanarishvara Shiva gave him a third leg, which helped him to regain his blood and strength.

In the context of Ardhanarishvara, we need to understand that a husband's wife is called Sangini, which means the partner of life. In the South Asian region, a wife is also called Ardhagini of the husband. It signifies that they are a half portion of their husband.

CHAPTER 4

Innocence on Shiva's face

One of the most attractive aspects of Shiva is his innocence. There are countless devotees of Lord Shiva who call him Bholenath. It is the most loved name of the Lord, which signifies the simplicity and grace of Lord Shiva.

It is fascinating to know that; there are no strict rules, traditions to worship Shiva. Lord Shiva is free from every infirmity, and everybody is free to worship him. No need to make any special arrangement for worshipping Shiva.

A single Bilva leaf is enough if offered with reverence.

Another most impressive thing about Shiva is, he is an admirer of his devotees. People also call him Baba.

In the Asian subcontinent, Baba means father figure. With immense love and devotion, Shiva devotees call him Baba Kedar or Baba Bholenath.

Shiva is transcendental; Lord Shiva is exceptional, where other deities wear expensive clothes with golden robes and live a glorious life.

Shiva believes in simplicity and inner peace. Anyone can connect with him easily; Shiva is always available for his devotees.

There are many lessons people can learn from Lord Shiva. But most people admire the simplicity of Lord Shiva.

Shiva wears the Rudraksha garland, Mrigshaala (Deerskin), and lives a Yogic life at Mount Kailash. He Smears dead bodies ash and holds a trident in his right hands.

Shiva likes to roam from one cremation ground to another without bothering about his divinity. Shiva is the creator, as well as the creation.

He is the one who is forever pure and Kind.

Once upon a time, Prajapati Daksha organized a massive gathering of the dignified people of the world.

Everyone decided to participate in it, and on the request of Lord Shiva devotees, Lord Shiva promised to participate in it.

The day before the gathering, Narada entered the Kailash. He informed Shiva that his brother, Prajapati Daksha is planning a conspiracy against Shiva.

In answer to that, Lord Shiva replied that if anyone hates me. It is their problem, not mine. I cannot hate anyone; everyone is dear to me, Narad. I cannot differentiate people on the grounds of their origin and Karma.

There is a beautiful Story of Shiva and Parvati which reveals the simplicity of Lord Shiva.

As we all know, Shiva and Parvati have immense love for each other. Shiva waited for many yugas for Goddess Parvati, who is the manifestation of Goddess Shakti.

It was the time when Shiva accepted the vairagya after getting separated from Goddess Sati. Shiva never expected anyone else other than Goddess Shakti.

Still, when Goddess Parvati approached Shiva for getting married to him, Shiva rejected Goddess Parvati at first.

After performing the penance on Shiva for several divine years Shiva finally accepted the love of goddess Parvati.

During the austerity Goddess, Parvati came out of human limitation and obtained her sublime form. For making that union successful, it was essential for Goddess Parvati to attain her divinity.

This section of their story showcases the simplicity of Lord Shiva, which is admirable in all aspects.

The most cherished daughter of Mountain King Himavan, Goddess Parvati, was dear to everyone in the family.

She was the soft princess raised with all the care. But the lifestyle of Lord Shiva was rigid and unorthodox.

After the rigorous penance on Shiva, Goddess Parvati wins the heart of Shiva. The King and queen get delighted to hear that. They give their consent for the marriage.

In Vaikuntha, Lord Vishnu was delighted with the news of the wedding. At Kailash, everyone gets happy to hear the joyful words of the Himavan. Then Lord Vishnu comes to meet Lord Shiva along with Brahma and demigods.

Lord Shiva was aware of the reason behind their arrival.

Still, Shiva requests Lord Vishnu to reveal the purpose of his arrival with Brahma. Lord Vishnu expresses his happiness for Parvati and Shiva's wedding. It was the moment of Shiva and Shakti for which everyone waited so long.

Lord Vishnu reminds everyone that after the divine wedding, Himavan will attain salvation. In the future, it could create disturbing circumstances for the earth.

 Brahaspati, the guru of demigods, says if Shiva can mock himself in front of Himavan. Then, after listening to harsh words for Shiva, king Himavan will get into the complex predicament about Shiva.

Due to their perplexity about Shiva, Himavan will never be able to get Moksha. Meanwhile, Bull Nandi, along with ShivGans, rejects the proposal of demigods.

Nandi warns everyone that it could create tightness for Shiva and goddess weddings. Nandi requests Shiva to refuse the suggestion.

Shiva smiles and looks at Nandi & Ganas with great affection. Shiva tells them my Aradhya Narayan and devas came here to discuss social welfare.

Some specific people's accountability towards society is more crucial than attaining Moksha.

Nandi requests Lord Shiva to explain in brief.

Shiva politely explains that few people in this world cannot get free of their responsibilities. Himavan is one of those people. Hence I will put King and queen into the dilemma.

Nandi reminds everyone what will happen if due to the dilemma, this wedding gets into the problem?

Shiva tells Nandi that due to the personal loss, he cannot avoid the responsibility of doing people's welfare. Indra and other demigods get happy, but Nandi was worried about the decision of Shiva.

The next day, at the Himavan's palace, Shiva appears as a Brahmin, and Nandi as a pupil of the Brahmin. Shiva, as a Brahmin, asks a question to Himavan, why are you marrying your dear daughter with that Aghori?

A man who likes to wear the garland of the skulls, roams in the jungle, ghosts are his friends and holds a trident.

He even has a snake on his neck. Do you know he loves to roam in the various cremation grounds? Nobody knows about his father.

How can you give your innocent daughter's hand to him?

Shiva is known as the greatest Kapali, and Ghost dances around him, and he loves to dance for destruction.

Himavan, the most important thing is, your family is Vaishnav, and Lord Vishnu is your Aradhya.

Then, how could you give your daughter to that Kapali?

Jaya informs Parvati about the Brahmin arrival and describes how Brahmin is defaming Shiva?

For a moment, Parvati thinks and then starts smiling. Parvati tells them we must welcome them with great honor in our palace.

They have come from far snowy mountains. They may be thirsty and hungry; we should cook some food for them.

Afterward, Parvati comes to the place where Brahmin and his pupil were mocking Shiva. Parvati slowly moves near towards Nandi and Shiva.

Firstly, Nandi noticed mother coming towards them.

He stops defaming Shiva; Nandi gets scared a little bit and takes a step backward. Unaware of goddess entry, Shiva, as a Brahmin, keeps insulting himself.

Parvati says, seer, Lord Vishnu blessed my entire family for this marriage. Narayan told us that he is delighted with the wedding of his Aradhya with me.

Hence, at this wedding, he will fulfill all the responsibilities of my elder brother. In a daunting voice, goddess Parvati requests Brahmin for breakfast.

Meanwhile, Himavan also requests Brahmin to eat some fruits and drink water first. But Nandi starts shivering with fear and stays there in his place.

Parvati takes Brahmin with him in the dining hall. The greatest destroyer of wickedness, Lord of the Lords, gets nervous; he becomes silent.

Parvati offers sweets to Shiva in a bowl and Lord Shiva silently picks some. Bhole was not looking at goddess Parvati. When Shiva starts having the sweets, she suddenly starts scolding Mahadev.

Parvati asks why you keep thinking about others' welfare every time. You even forgot that you have not yet become the son-in-law of the state.

Think for a moment, how will my mother react, if she will hear all that?

You just came here to slander yourself without thinking about me, and one thing more, I will not leave that Nandi too.

How dare he not stop you; he impulsively follows you everywhere. You have done enough welfare of people.

Time has come to think about us, Mahadev. Shiva looks at the big eyes of goddess Parvati and says. It was not Nandi's fault, my dear, Uma.

Nandi reminded me of all that, please forgive him; it was my fault.

When Shiva said that, he kept lots of love in his eyes for the goddess. The heart of the goddess melted after seeing the charm of Lord Shiva.

After that, both looked at each other with love. Parvati says, what are you looking for, Lord?

Shiva says, Uma, I'm getting nourished with your immense affection.

Parvati puts her eyeballs down and again scolds Shiva to eat sweets.

The god of the gods again starts eating his sweets.

Parvati requests Shiva to take the original form in which she likes him the most. To fulfill the wish of Parvati, Bholenath takes the form of Shiva.

She gets happy to see Shiva in the prime form. With so much humility, Shiva promises that soon he will bring Baraat to her palace.

CHAPTER 5

The greatest giver of Peace, health, and fortune

Shiva is the first god in the Sanatan dharma, known as Adidev. It implies that Shiva is the preVedic Lord, the Lord before the Vedic era. Lord Shiva cannot be comparable to anyone in any aspect.

Shiva is a Moksha giver who puts you on the path of righteousness.

He is Shaktipati; he is superior, unconquerable, and infinite. Just by chanting his auspicious mantra, people's suffering starts disappearing.

Those people who revere Shiva have enormous energy, focus, and skill. The limitless dynamism of Lord Shiva can be experienced by chanting these powerful mantras.

These mantras are 100 percent practical and can be chant by anyone.

Most importantly, negativity will not be able to harm you. Chanters of the Shiva mantra will experience focus with joy.

Sage Markandeya formulated moksha giver Maha Mrityunjaya Mantra of Lord Shiva. Troubles and all sorts of sorrows stay away from those people who harmonize Vedic mantras.

Chanting Hanuman Chalisa and Mahamrityunjaya Mantra on a routine basis has many health benefits.

The Maha Mrityunjaya mantra removes the fear of instant death and liberates from all sorts of difficulties.

Chanting this mantra prevents you from unexpected death.

This mantra is also known as **Rudra Mantra**, **Beej mantra**, or **Tryambakaṁ Mantra**. Chanting the Mahamrityunjaya Mantra 1008 times is considered highly favorable. It brings good luck, health, and prosperity.

Chanting Mahamrityunjaya mantra on Mondays is considered more beneficial than other days.

Here is the mantra.

Tryambakam yajamahe sugandhiṁ pusti-vardhanam |

Urvarukam-iva bandhanatmrtyormuksiya mamrtat

Here is the meaning of the mantra

We worship the three-eyed supreme god (Shiva), who is aromatic. He is the one who nourishes and nurtures all beings.

As the developed cucumber automatically drops from its note, may Lord Shiva redeem us from the fear of death for the sake of immortality?

Chanting Maha Mrityunjaya mantra in the early morning is desirable by ancient Yogis and sages. In case if anyone in your home is going through any set of problems.

Advise them to chant Mahamrityunjaya Mantra. It will help them to overcome their problem.

Anybody can chant the Maha Mrityunjaya Mantra. Even pregnant ladies are free to chant the mantra; they will find it helpful in their deliveries.

If you are going through a lack of sleep disorder, start chanting Mahamrityunjaya Mantra or Panchakshari mantra **OM NAMAH SHIVAYA**.

It will help you to reduce your stress and neutralize the sleeping disorder.

Lord Shiva is the greatest giver of health and fortune. By chanting the Lord Shiva mantras, you can unlock all the happiness in your life.

Dear friend, if you think any magic will happen by chanting the Lord Shiva mantra is a wrong approach towards eternal blissfulness.

Indeed, the Shiva mantra creates the energy within; a positive vibration will release in your mind and body.

It activates the inactive neurons and energy junction of the brain and body.

The vibrational energy passes into the spinal cord and merges to Sushmna (Nadi), where the Muladhara chakra lies. It opens the door of possibilities for you in Dhyaan (Meditation).

After that process, the significant transformation takes place to the body and mind of the chanter.

1- Mantra chanting keeps negative energies away from your house. Your life will become blissful; you will start feeling more strength within you.

2- If mantra chanted with pure devotion towards Shiva, things would turn in your favor. You start attracting health, wealth, and success.

3 - Mantra helps the chanter to create a protective shield around them. Lord Shiva himself becomes the protector of the chanter. The positivity starts emitting from that house people.

4 - Disorder like fear, anxiety, and depression starts disappearing. You will feel more fresh and calm. The positive energies of divinity get established in the people of that house.

5 - Shiva mantra like Om Namah Shivaya calms the human mind and gives tranquility. It also helps yogis to invoke their Shiva- Shakti inside them.

6 - From a health perspective, Shiva Mantra stabilizes the heartbeat of the person and Increases the metabolism process within them. Your medical condition will start improving; your respiration will improve. Impure blood will begin to purify by the proper functioning of arteries and veins. Hence,

your skin will start glowing naturally.

7 - Worshipping Shiva will put you on the path of righteousness and faith, which will further take you to the path of Moksha. You will get filled with positivity in your life.

According to Shiva Purana, those who chant the Shiva mantra, wear the beads of the Rudraksha necklace and apply three horizontal lines known as Tripunda.

Even Yamraaj (the death deity) cannot harm those mantra chanters.

Demon king Ravan was one of the greatest devotees of Lord Shiva. He was aware that if he could personalize Lord Shiva, he would become invincible.

Due to worshipping Shiva, Ravan acquired almost everything. He had golden Lanka, immense strength, wealth, and lethal weapons.

All the celestial beings were at his mercy, whereas, due to his ego, Shiva decided to free his devotee Ravan from the disorder of ego.

The name of Lord Rama is too dear to Lord Shiva. Both Shiva and Rama consider each other their gods and devotees.

Lord Rama worshipped Shiva all his life as his Aradhya. Similarly, the name of Lord Rama is so delightful for Lord Shiva.

On the other hand, Ravan ignored Lord Rama; by considering him an ordinary man.

Before the war between Lord Rama and demon king Ravana, Lord Rama worshipped Shiva with humility and gained strength from Shiva.

As a result, Shri Rama defeated Ravan and gave Lanka to Vibhishana. At the end of his life, Ravan realized, you cannot achieve Shiva if your intentions are not good.

It was the Guru Mantra that Ravana gave to the Laxman, younger brother of Lord Rama.

After believing in Shiva, you will become compassionate, calm, dynamic, uncomplicated, and joyful.

When you start growing these qualities within you in that time, you become eligible for getting all the delight.

It is the state of eternal bliss; it is the state of Shivoham in which a person is free from all the negativities and worldly desires.

CHAPTER 6

Shiva acted Unbiased [Deliver justice to everyone]

Yes, Shiva never differentiated anyone based on caste, origin, and gender. It is the reason everyone kept trust in him. From time to time, various Asura misinterpreted Lord Shiva's innocence.

For elaborating it, let me share two short stories.

Demon Tarakasura was a devotee of Shiva and blessed by a benefit that only Shiva's son can kill him. He was aware that Shiva is Vairagi, who will never get married to any lady. Therefore, there was no chance of his death.

Things get changed for Tarakasura when Shiva gets married to Goddess Sati, the manifestation of Shakti. He gets frightened by the Shiva and Sati marriage. Tarakasura had a powerful son, his name was Vidyunmali.

At the request of his son, Tarakasura reveals his fear of getting killed by Shiva's son. Taking note of that, Vidyunmali decides to do austerity on Shiva. At Kailash, Shiva was sitting with Sati when Vidyunmali started his penance.

One Day, Shiva tells Sati that he has to go and grant the boon to Asur son, Vidyunmali. Before going, Shiva says, now you have to look after Kailash. At that moment, Sati doesn't understand the meaning of Shiva's word.

On the other hand, Shiva appears in front of Vidyunmali and asks to take any boon.

Shiva says, Vidyunmali, I'm happy with your austerity, son; you can ask your desired wish.

Vidyunmali politely says, oh great lord; I want you to always stay with me. I have a threat to my life from my enemy; I want you to guard my life. Shiva gives the boon of Vidyunmali and agrees to defend him as his protector.

Many days pass, Sati keeps wondering why Shiva didn't return to Kailash. Nandi informs Sati that Lord Shiva is defending Vidyunmali as his protector.

Goddess Sati asks Nandi why Shiva is doing that.

Nandi replies that in his boon, Vidyunmali asked Shiva to protect him from external threats. Sati gets angry at Vidyunmali and decides to go to Asura palace to meet Shiva.

After reaching there, Shiva informs goddess Sati that now he is protecting Vidyunmali as his guard.

Hence cannot come back to Kailash. Vidyunmali welcomes Goddess Sati with great humility, but Sati gets angry at Vidyunmali.

Sati says, how dare you to captivate Shiva as your defender. Don't you know Shiva is boundless? Why did you trick him?

Vidyunmali says Shiva vowed to protect me as my guard. Now, I have rights on Shiva, and I cannot allow Shiva to go back to Kailash.

Sati gets angry at that and says, Vidyunmali, you remembered that Shiva is your protector, but forgot that Shiva and Shakti are inseparable.

As I'm the consort of Shiva, I have the right to stay with my husband.

Now from today, I will stay here with Shiva. Vidyunmali, you are obligated to take care of your guard's family.

Therefore Vidyunmali makes proper arrangements for your guard's family.

Vidyunmali says he is not responsible for taking care of his guard's family.

Sati takes the grand Adishakti form, and Vidyunmali gets scared by viewing that. He tries to snatch the trident from Shiva's hand.

 But he starts getting buried on earth under the weight of Shiva's trident.

In the grand form of Adishakti, Sati says, you fool, don't you know only Shiva and Shakti can bear the weight of Shiva's trident?'' No one else in the entire universe has the strength to lift Shiva's trident.

Meanwhile, Tarakasura comes there and requests Shiva to bless Vidyunmali as his stupid son. Tarakasura orders Vidyunmali to free Shiva from the vow.

Vidyunmali gets confused that if he allows Shiva and Sati to live there, it will become easy for Shiva's son to kill Tarakasura. Vidyunmali frees Shiva from his promise, and Shiva requests Sati to get back to her soft form.

Sati gets back to her peaceful form, and Vidyunmali seeks an apology from

Shiva and Sati. Shiva and Sati forgive them and return to Kailash. Later Shiva's son Kartikeya killed Tarakasura.

Another story of Bhasmasura simplifies the concept of Shiva Unbiased actions.

The story of Bhasmasura gives a vital moral lesson to everyone that you cannot attain Siddhis without overcoming your inner darkness like ego, passion, anger, illusion, and lust.

If you still try to get siddhis without awakening spirituality within, these Siddhis will burn you out.

Let's know, who was Bhasmasura?

A long time ago, there was a demon named Bruk, the son of Shakuni. Since birth, Bruks was a foolish son to his parents. Due to his stupidity, he always kept creating obstacles for his father.

One day his father criticized him that he will never achieve success or anything in his life.

Bruk realized that his father never expected him to become successful.

Therefore, he decides to prove wrong his father that he is not a stupid son. He was desperate to prove himself successful, but he had no idea how to do that?

One day Sage Narada informed him to worship Shiva and take boons from

Shiva. Narada tells him that Shiva is kind and it is easy to please Lord Shiva.

Stupid Bruk takes the advice of sage Narada and starts searching for a peaceful place for him where he could peacefully meditate on Lord Shiva.

Fortunately, he finds a place in the center of the forest where he could meditate on Shiva.

Many years pass, one day Brahma, and Vishnu meet Shiva at Mount Kailash. Lord Narayan tells Lord Shiva that time has come to bless a boon to demon Bruk.

Lord Shiva gives his consent that Bruk got a chance in his life; now, he has to decide for himself.

Shiva elaborates that if a devotee's feeling is genuine; then, he doesn't require any boon. Lord Narayan agrees on that, and Shiva goes to meet Bruk.

Brahma asks Lord Vishnu, Narayana, are you ready?

Lord Vishnu tells, Yes, Lord Brahma, I'm ready.

Lord Shiva appears in front of the demon Bruk and requests him to open his eyes.

Demon Bruk gets delighted to see his lord in front of him. Bruk falls into the feet of Shiva and starts weeping.

Shiva informs Bruk that he has successfully performed his penance. Now he has the right to ask anything from Shiva as the boon.

Bruk tells Shiva that his father always treated him as an idiotic and failed son. But today, he could tell his father and other people that he has got success in his penance.

Lord Shiva asks Bruk to ask something in return for his austerity. Demon Bruk gets overwhelmed for a moment; and thinks, what is the most precious in life?

Bruk tells Shiva that he needs some moment for himself so that he could think properly. Shiva accepts the demon's request and sits over a rock there.

Lord Shiva lets Bruk think about his wish. The Asur tells Shiva that he has no idea about what kind of boon he should ask from Shiva?

Shiva recommends Asur that he can make him sensible if he wants.

Bruk refuses the advice of Shiva by saying that he already proved everybody wrong.

Bruk tells Shiva that everybody should fear him. He needs some unique power that no one ever had.

Asur requests Shiva to bless him with the ability to turn anyone into ashes. He says, as soon as I put my hand on others' heads, they should get turned into ash.

Shiva gives the blessing to the Bruk, but the Asur tells Shiva that he will examine Shiva's boon.

Shiva says he is sitting there till Bruk returns. Asur goes to the jungle and sees some wild buffalos; he puts his hand on their head.

Buffalo immediately turns into ashes. Bruk realizes that Shiva has given him the exact boon. Now, Asur decides to test the penance benefit on people. Bruk goes into the ashram and sees rishis performing Vedic rituals.

Bruk puts his hand over a sage head and burns him out. Immediately, one of the sage screams, Bhasmasura is here, protect your life.

Bruk hears the shout of sages and likes his new name Bhasmasura. Then he decided to test the boon on devas (demigods) and appear on Swarg (heaven).

Demigods get scared after seeing Bhasmasura there; they run out from the Swarga. That gives happiness to Asur Bhasmasura.

It was the first time people were noticing him and getting frightened of him.

 Now after conquering Swarga, he desires a beautiful woman with whom he could share his success.

Bhasmasura sees Goddess Parvati and thinks that he needs to burn Lord Shiva by putting his hand over Shiva's head.

Lord Shiva was seeing everything, whatever Bhasmasura was doing.

Asur returns to Shiva and gives thanks to Shiva for the benefit. He tells Shiva that now he wants to take Mahadev's place. To do that, he has to put his hand on Shiva's head.

Shiva says, Bhasmasura, I hope you enjoyed your new powers. If you want to examine your new strength on me, you are welcome, Bhasmasura. I'm right here sitting on this rock.

Bhasmasura starts running towards Shiva, and Shiva closes his eyes and starts meditation. In the Dhyana Yoga, Shiva reduces the speed of Kaal Chakra (wheel of time).

The pace of Bhasmasura towards Shiva gets remarkably low. Reaching up to Shiva becomes impossible for Asur.

It was the perfect time for Lord Vishnu to appear in the back of Bhasmasura. Lord Vishnu comes in the appearance of a beautiful lady.

On the other side, Shiva increases the speed of the Kaal chakra for the Asur.

As soon as time restarts for Asur, Bhasmasura hears the voice of a beautiful woman. He looks at her; she tells her name **Mohini**.

Bhasmasura forgets about Shiva and tells Mohini that she is a beautiful woman.

He was willing to make her his queen. Asur introduces himself by the name of Bhasmasura. Mohini says to Asura that he seems to be powerful, but he cannot impress her with his power.

A man who could perform precisely the same mudra (position) in dancing as she does could win her heart.

Bhasmasura agrees with Mohini and starts dancing. After watching her dance, Bhasmasura starts copying her dance moves.

Bhasmasura was enjoying every dance step. He was trying to match his dancing moves exactly with Mohini.

Finally, while dancing, Mohini puts the right hand on her head and Bhasmasura also does that. As a result, Bhasmasura burns out and turns into ashes.

CHAPTER 7

The Destroyer of Darkness

At the highest level, Shiva is limitless, transcendental, unchanging, and formless. In his physical appearance, Shiva has a winsome persona.

The one whose shine is brighter than millions of sun, and the one who is master of panch Mahabhoot still own no roof over his head. He is also known as the greatest warrior of all time.

He loves to live in the freezing conditions of Kailash with his family and takes care of his devotees everywhere in the cosmos.

The world has given him the name of the greatest destroyer, but only his devotees know what he is for them.

Shiva is the one who has never tricked anyone and did what he promised. Demons, demigods, sages, animals, nature, humans showed their trust in him.

Lord Shiva is also the one who is known for his destructive abilities. But in the other perspective, Lord Shiva has a compassionate nature.

It is remarkable to understand why a destroyer is admired and worshipped by everyone.

Once upon a time, the king of the demigods Indra crosses the limitations of his ego. He started ignoring everyone in the arrogance of his strength.

He even insults Gurudev, Brihaspati. In the arrogance, Indra says, there is no use of having a guru on Swarga.

Shiva notices the ego of Indra and decides to free Indra from that disorder as Indra was the king of the demigods.

In the appearance of an Aghori, Shiva sits on the path of Indra. The king of demigods Indra sees a stranger Aghori, resting in the middle of the path.

He orders Aghori to give him the way. Aghori says he is too old to move from his position. If Indra likes, he can cross over him.

Indra gets angry at Aghori and says if he doesn't move. He will throw him out of the way.

Aghori tells Indra that he will be grateful to Indra if he does that.
Indra decides to lift the Aghori and throw him far away.

He applied his incredible strength to lift Aghori, but the old weaker Aghori didn't move. Indra thinks how is that possible?

How a weaker sage could be so heavy? Indra starts realizing that he could not be an ordinary Aghori, so he folds his hand with humility, and asks who are you, seer?

Indra also realizes that he has limited knowledge, and he shouldn't be insulting his Guru. Self-realization tears come from his eyes.

From behind, Brihaspati's voice tells Indra that old Sage is none other than infinite Shiva. Indra gets happy to hear the Brihaspati voice.

Now Shiva takes his auspicious form, but Indra gets confused about whom he should respect first. Brihaspati understands the confusion of Indra and orders him to be grateful for Shiva as Shiva destroyed the ego of Indra.

Indra does exactly; he bows down to Shiva first, then his Guru, Brihaspati.

Another great story is of Goddess Parvati before her marriage with Lord Shiva. It was the time when Lord Shiva freed Goddess Parvati from her ego.

The story is like this.

It is the story of goddess Parvati before her marriage with Lord Shiva. Parvati used to worship Shiva with flowers, milk, honey, fruits, and sweets like Kheer.

She believed that her way of worshipping Shiva is the best way of worshipping Shiva.

One day while collecting fruits and flowers for her evening prayers. She saw a few Aghoris wearing Rudraksha worshipping Shiva with fresh flesh.

Aghoris were offering meat on the lingam. When Parvati sees Aghori doing that, she becomes furious at them.

Parvati stopped them by doing so. She aggressively scolded them for their worshipping style.

Aghori smiled and politely told Parvati that they don't know any Shiva mantras or verses to please Shiva. The only mantra they know is Om Namah Shivaya.

That's why they are chanting Om Namah Shivaya every time they offer flesh to Shiva lingam. Parvati described that it is not appropriate to worship Shiva's lingam with flesh.

Shiva will never accept tamasic flesh. Aghoris answered that Shiva takes the parts of meat and consumes it whenever they offer it to the lingam.

Parvati gets surprised, and Aghoris offers a fresh piece of flesh on lingam in front of her, and meat disappears as Shiva is consuming it.

Now, Aghori invites Parvati to worship Shiva. Parvati tells them that she wants a distinct Lingam. On that, Aghori says that lingam is a lingam.

There is no difference in them, and she can use Aghori's lingam.
Parvati brings beautiful white flowers, fruits and offers them on the lingam.

Flowers and fruits remain the same on the lingam. Parvati gets silent and asks Aghoris why Shiva consumed their tamasic meat pieces but not her fruits?

Aghoris tells, you judged our way of worshipping Shiva and assumed yourself more influential than us.

It is the ego that continues inside you, Princess. You have to come out of it.

Shiva is free from the conventional way of worshipping. There are no specific laws to worship Shiva, and everyone is free to worship Shiva. For Shiva, every devotee is equivalent to him.

Believing that your way of worshipping is better than others is not the path that takes you to the Shiva.

The only thing which is required is genuine devotion and faith in Shiva. It is most significant while worshipping Shiva.

Parvati admits her mistake and gives thanks to the group of the Aghoris for enlightening her. She returns to her palace and decides to attain her Sadhvi Form. The group of Agoris was Sapta rishis, and their leader was Lord Shiva.

CHAPTER 8

Unorthodox Shiva

Lord Shiva is unconventional in the basic approach. Everything about Shiva makes him different from others. He is the Lord with no start and endpoint and represents the absolute voidness from which the universe emerges and goes back in the end.

The unique things are dear to Lord Shiva. It is the reason snakes, cremation ground ghost, Datura all are an internal part of Shiva consciousness.

The devotees of other deities offer them sweets and flowers. On the other side, devotees of Shiva offer weed and toxic substances to Shiva.

Shiva is the ultimate source of all auspiciousness of the world. But, Shiva devotees offer toxic substances to Shiva. They do it because they want Shiva to consume their past sins and give them liberation from bad karmas as Shiva consumed the Halahal to protect the universe from the deadly poison.

He is not a materialistic Lord. Shiva never does anything by himself. Other deities are appointed to take care of everything, whereas Shiva lives a vairagyi lifestyle. He is a dispassionate man who is far away from worldly desires.

One can understand it by example.

Yama, the death deity, manages the ratio of death and birth on earth.

Similarly, the Shani deity (Saturn Planet) serves justice based on the Karma of people. Likewise, Varun, Kaamdev, and many have distinct responsibilities.

Every deity has some set of responsibilities to which they are restricted. But Shiva is free from every obligation, rule, and tradition. It is the reason Lord Shiva is known as Supreme Vairagi.

Shiva never actively engages in anything; all the Shiva tasks are done by his fearsome forms, like Rudra and Bhairavas. There are different forms of Shiva, like Rudra to Shankar.

Therefore, Shiva is an unpredictable Lord of the Lords. Shiva dancing form is known as Natraj. In that form, Shiva expresses the process of creation and destruction.

Natraj, the dancing form of Shiva explains the concept of dancing energy, mass, and matter dynamics in the scientific aspect.

 In the global outlook of every phenomenon, Lord Vishnu is responsible for taking care of everything. He is the ultimate preserver. On the other side, Shiva is the ultimate destroyer who merges everything in him.

Many things make Lord Shiva the coolest Lord of the Lords. Not discriminating against people on the grounds of their Karma is one of them.

Shiva is the master in every art, like dancing, playing musical instruments, war skills, and many more. Lord Shiva can effortlessly turn any adverse condition in his favor. It makes him more attractive and knowledgeable.

It is the art of persuasion; those people who are masters in this art can achieve so much in their lives without applying max effort.

If you could get this art in your life, you can achieve tremendous success in business and the job that you are pursuing.

Now let us understand this quality of Shiva how he turns adverse conditions in his favor.

As we know, goddess Sati was the first consort of Shiva; she was the manifestation of goddess Adishakti.

 Adishakti was born as the daughter of Prajapati Daksha; Sage Narada named the little girl goddess Sati. When princess Sati grew up, she fell in love with Shiva.

The amount of love goddess Sati received from her father Daksha was unconditional, but her father Daksha was one of the biggest haters of Shiva.

The vital part of the story was that his dear daughter Sati was in love with Vairagi Shiva. Sati goes against her father's will and marries Lord Shiva.

Vijaya, the elder sister of Sati, always had envy for Sati.

When Vijaya comes to know that Sati is married to a yogi who wears

Rudraksha as the ornament, and there is a snake over the neck of Shiva. She gets delighted.

Vijaya assumes Sati is married to the wrong person, and she misinterprets Shiva in every aspect. She thinks that Sati has chosen the wicked husband for herself.

She wonders how a girl can choose such a man who smears cremation ground ashes and lives an ascetic lifestyle. Vijaya decides to capitalize on the situation of the newly married couple.

For that, Vijaya decides to organize a grand supper for the newly married couple Shiva and Sati.

As we all know, Mahadev lives a unique lifestyle and doesn't know much about worldly rituals. Shiva believes in uprightness, which is why Shiva is known as Bholenath.

It was a grand feast organized by Sati's elder sister, and the world has never seen something that luxurious. In the evening, the fest started by Vijaya. All devotees reach there, including Shiva Gans.

After joining the dining hall, Shiva gans acts surprised by viewing the beauty and arrangement made.

It was the first time they had seen something that beautiful and delicious at the same time. The smell of the tasty dishes was reaching their noses, which was making them impatient.

Bull Nandi orders them to stay within their limits and follow all the traditions of the guest. Vijaya finds it amusing that Shivgans are getting impatient for supper; she calls Sati to take care of the supper.

Sati decides to serve food to Shiva Gans and dignitaries present over there. Sati reaches near to the Shivgans with her utensil filled with Kheer. The sweet smells of Sati's utensil increase their appetite.

Shivgans grab the container of Kheer and start eating with bare hands. Nandi tries to control them, but their nature was chaotic.

Goddess Sati gets shocked by seeing the weird behavior of Shivagans. Shiva Gans were fighting with each other. Demigods and dignitaries present over there were watching everything from their corners.

The whole situation gets out of control, and the goddess Sati feels depressed by seeing that ShivaGans don't know how to behave on the meal organized for them.

Meanwhile, Shiva appears there with a pleasing smile on his face and sees all his Gans. Goddess Sati comes toward Shiva and asks Shiva to observe the whole situation.

Sati says, Look, Swami, What ShivGans are doing there?

Shiva sees his Gans with immense affection and love and then replies to Goddess Sati.

Shiva says, Sati, they are enjoying your hospitality; what else?

Look at them, feel the expression of happiness on their faces. Your meal fulfilled their appetite. It is the happiness of children who are enjoying the food served by their mother.

Sati sees Shiva's eyes, and Shiva gives a smile to the goddess, and then Mahakaal moves toward his Gans and reaches in between them.

Shiva accepts salutations of the dignitaries present over there.

Shiva starts walking towards them. Shiva Gan gets more excited and makes a place for Shiva by clearing the mess.

Sati sees Shiva in between his Gans. An expression of calmness comes to Sati's eyes. She realizes what Shiva indeed represents.

She understands the innocence and simplicity of Shiva.

Shiva tells Sati.

Shiva, Sati, by seeing them, I'm feeling to join them in this supper, and enjoy the food cooked by you for us.

An apparition brings the food on a plate for Shiva, and Shiva sits there.

Shankara looks at Sati and requests Sati to join him and take a food bite.

Sati sees, here and there; everybody was looking at her.

Then, Sati looks at Shiva. Her eyeball gets down with a pleasant smile on her face.

Slowly, she steps toward Shiva and sits next to him. Everyone present over there chants Om Namah Shivaya and Har Har Mahadev!

Shiva sees the goddess with immense love and offers a food bite with his hands. Sati takes the food bite from Shiva's hand and then offers a food bite to Shiva with her hand.

Narayan was looking from the door with Laxmi. Both smile and get happy to see Shiva and Shakti together. Everyone present there chants Har Har Mahadev. Sage Kashyap requests everybody to get the Prasada of Shiva. The joys & celebration continue.

It is a gentle quality of Shiva, which can turn any adverse situation into an emphatic circumstance. Anybody can learn that quality of Shiva.

CHAPTER 9

Harmony, friendship, and diversity

Lord Shiva is the complete Lord in every aspect. What makes Shiva most loved God is the persona he carries of a family man. Shiva lives in Kailash, and Goddess Parvati is his consort.

Lord Kartikeya and Lord Ganesha are the two sons of Shiva. Lord Shiva also has a daughter whose name is Devi Ashok Sundari.

Shiva always looked after his family as the ordinary man takes care of the family. Shiva Shankar fulfilled every responsibility as head of the family.

There was a time when the family of Lord Shiva was going through some unrest. The elder son of Shiva, Lord Kartikeya, was upset with the few decisions of the family.

But Shiva intelligently solved the problem by making Lord Kartikeya realize that he is as significant as Ganesha.

Apart from that, Lord Ganesha also expressed his affection for the elder brother, Kartikeya.

The beautiful part of Kailash is there are snakes, peacocks, rats, tigers, bulls, and other creatures. Everyone lives in harmony without creating trouble for others. Humanity can learn the lesson of compassion and grace from them.

Shiva is Lord of the Lords, known as the originator of various art and skill. Therefore be like Shiva, an explorer, creator, preserver, and destroyer of the darkness and evil ideology.

Apart from that, Shiva is the greatest friend, guru, and Aradhya for Lord Vishnu. Similarly, Lord Vishnu is a great companion, guru, and aradhya of Shiva.

Once, Shiva presented himself as Harihar, which means half Vishnu and half Shiva. The message behind that avatar was to demonstrate that it is wrong to compare Shiva and Vishnu. Both are collectively one.

Worshipping anyone means automatically worshipping another one. Once Shiva also said that I live in the heart of Vishnu, and Lord Vishnu lives in my heart.

Therefore, it doesn't matter whom you worship; ultimately, you worship the one supreme consciousness.

Thank you

I appreciate you for taking your precious time to buy, and read this book. It means a lot. Please, feel free for writing your reviews.

Have a great day ahead and keep smiling. You can connect with me on all the major social media platforms. And details are available in the Author section of the book.

Regards

Santosh Gairola

About Author

Santosh Gairola is the author of the Book. He is an Indian who loves to write about Fictional stories, positivity, motivation, and spirituality. The author firmly believes that we are divine, and there is Shiva tattva within everyone.

Here is the author's contact information.

Email –

Developer.santosh@live.in

Website –

https://www.Viyali.com/

Facebook –

1) Facebook Author page - https://www.facebook.com/AuthorSantoshGairola

2) Facebook Profile page - https://www.facebook.com/samy.santosh

Instagram

https://www.instagram.com/author.santosh.gairola/

Twitter's Handler –

https://twitter.com/Viyalifounder

If you have any suggestions, feel free to send me. I will be thankful for all your kind suggestions.

THANK YOU, KEEP SMILING

LIFE IS BEAUTIFUL!!
HAR HAR MAHADEV

Printed in Great Britain
by Amazon

45460470R00046